CONTENTS

INTRODUCTION

You might be wondering why we are writing about a "container" in the context of achieving results. Isn't that the purview of everyone's favorite, "The Container Store"? While we love that store, too, we think that the container is very important to results-based leadership (RBL) work, and is, in fact, a critical piece of creating successful RBL engagements.

RBL is a unique approach to leadership development that builds the core competencies in leaders that allow them to effectively drive toward results. RBL has two foundational skills: Results-Based Accountability (RBA), an approach used to differentiate between population- and program-level results, to use data to develop impactful strategies, and to establish ways of tracking whether the work is making a contribution to the achievement of results; and Results Based Facilitation (RBF), which helps leaders design, lead, and contribute in meetings that effectively move groups from talk to action and hold participants accountable for advancing the work.

The container is the infrastructure that supports results-based leaders as they meet to achieve the results they have designated. Without an adequate container, groups do not have the preparation, structure, support, or resources to get their important work done. Even with talented profession-als leading the meeting and committed participants, a sluggish container leads to less than optimal meeting results, which, in turn, makes it harder to achieve overall results for children, families, and other populations.

Many of you reading this book have attended an RBL workshop and/or are using RBL practices in your work on a daily basis. In order for you to fully implement your RBL knowledge in your home organization, you need to know the whys, hows, and whats of creating the container for the work — which is what this booklet is designed to do. Plus, we've included checklists to support your planning and help you hit the ground running.

One last note about the container: The concept of needing a container for successful RBL work was originally developed by Jolie Bain Pillsbury in "The Theory of Aligned Contributions." Many of the components of creating a container that we list in this booklet were developed by Pillsbury and are documented in her books, *Results Based Facilitation: Moving from Talk to Action, Book One and Book Two*. We are grateful to Pillsbury for the experience and scholarship that gave birth to these powerful concepts and tools, and for her generous sharing of them with many communities.

THE CONTAINER IS CREATED

THROUGHOUT

THE PROJECT

Creating the container to achieve results is not just about setting up the meeting room or ordering supplies. In contrast, it is an ongoing set of activities that begins with the launch of the project and continues until after the meeting, or set of meetings, is completed.

Creating the container is also a mindset, a way of strategically thinking about the group and project at hand — with an almost relentless focus on both — to provide a seamless infrastructure to help the group make progress toward the results they have identified to achieve. With that in mind, Figure 1 shows the phases of most RBL projects:

FIGURE 1

The steps for creating the container to achieve results are discussed in detail in the following pages of this booklet. A master checklist for the steps can be found in Appendix One.

LAUNCH

Launching the project is always exciting, but sometimes it is hard to know where to start. Below is a checklist of the important container-related steps to complete when you launch a project:

STEPS TO COMPLETE AT PROJECT LAUNCH

- ✖ SET MEETING DATE(S)
- ✖ IDENTIFY MEETING STAFFING
- ✖ GET STAFF CONTRACTS IN PLACE, IF APPLICABLE
- ✖ IDENTIFY MEMBERS OF THE IMPLEMENTATION TEAM AND CLARIFY ROLES
- ✖ RESERVE MEETING SPACE, INCLUDING THE AFTERNOON BEFORE THE MEETING SO THE ROOM CAN BE SET UP
- ✖ SEND "SAVE THE DATE" EMAIL TO MEETING PARTICIPANTS
- ✖ POST MEETING DATE AND PURPOSE ON SOCIAL MEDIA FORUMS, IF APPROPRIATE
- ✖ ARRANGE TRAVEL LOGISTICS FOR MEETING STAFF
- ✖ SET UP A SHARED FILE SYSTEM, IF APPROPRIATE
- ✖ SET DATES FOR TWO CO-DESIGN MEETINGS AND A FINAL CHECK-IN CALL

Set Meeting Date(s)

As implied by the heading title for this section, some projects will involve only one meeting, others several. The steps in this booklet can be applied to either type of project — just repeat the applicable steps as you go along if your project includes multiple meetings.

Identify Members of the Implementation Team

The "Implementation Team" is the group of individuals that will help plan, design, and execute the meeting. The composition and size of the Implementation Team varies depending on the size of the organization and the scope of the meeting. The team typically includes two to five people, such as the meeting facilitators and other staff, members from the sponsoring organization, and other stakeholders. Identifying members of the Implementation Team as part of the Project Launch ensures that the key people are involved in the entire process of creating a successful meeting and achieving the desired meeting results.

As part of forming the Implementation Team, it is always important to clarify roles to make sure everyone knows what work is theirs to do for the meeting. While each member of the Implementation Team has a role to play in creating the container, each role is very distinct and includes an agreed-upon set of tasks for that role. In RBL, this is referred to as "Boundaries of Authority/Role and Task, or B/ART."[1]

Select and Reserve the Meeting Space

Selecting the right space for the meeting is of key importance to achieving the meeting results! We can't stress this enough. The wrong meeting space can impede a group's work and reduce its productive output.

First and foremost: The room must have tables that can be moved around to accommodate different working configurations for the group. A Board Room with long, stationary tables is an example of the *least desirable* type of room. Instead, select a room with smaller tables that can be moved around to meet the group's needs as it works in affinity or discussion groups, pairs, or other configurations.

The room should be big enough to accommodate an open U seating arrangement for a smaller group, and a number of smaller tables in an arc-type shape for a larger group, both of which are illustrated below. If round tables are available, that is helpful.

**OPEN U SEATING ARRANGEMENT
FOR SMALLER GROUP**

TABLES ARRANGED FOR A LARGER GROUP

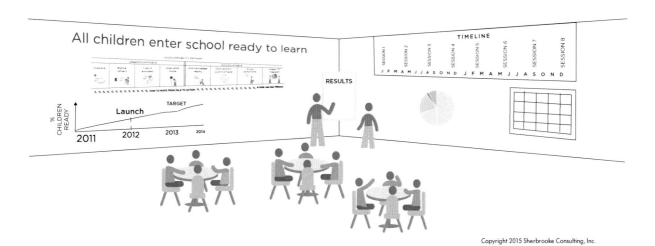

Copyright 2015 Sherbrooke Consulting, Inc.

If possible, select a room with natural light to help keep the group's energy "up." The room will also need to accommodate the data that the group will display, either taped up on an open wall or placed on a series of easels along a wall.

If at all possible, **arrange to have access to the meeting room the afternoon before the actual meeting.** This will allow the Implementation Team to set up the meeting room, place participant materials, hang data on the walls, and other preparatory steps. Having the room ready well before the meeting starts puts all the meeting sponsors and staff at ease and is a key factor in creating a container that will support meeting results.

Arrange Travel Logistics for Meeting Staff

It is important to do this step early if it is required for your meeting(s). If members of the Implementation Team cannot get their desired flights, then their work to support meeting results can be compromised. Key steps in arranging travel logistics include:

- Researching, proposing, and purchasing travel tickets
- Reserving hotel rooms
- Reserving rental cars
- Making any updates, changes, or cancellations along the way, as needed

THE
CO-DESIGN
PROCESS

As you may remember from your RBL workshop if you attended one, the Co-Design Process is essential to RBL work. Through the Co-Design Process, all members of the Implementation Team have the opportunity to help plan the meeting and provide necessary and helpful input to the meeting results, participants, and agenda.

STEPS TO COMPLETE DURING CO-DESIGN

- ✖ PROVIDE TEMPLATE FOR PARTICIPANT COMPOSITION ANALYSIS
- ✖ SEND PROPOSED AGENDA FOR FIRST CO-DESIGN MEETING WITH SUPPORTING MATERIALS, IF ANY
- ✖ HOLD THE FIRST CO-DESIGN MEETING
- ✖ SEND DRAFT ANNOTATED AGENDA TO IMPLEMENTATION TEAM AND PROPOSED AGENDA FOR SECOND CO-DESIGN MEETING
- ✖ HOLD THE SECOND CO-DESIGN MEETING
- ✖ SEND THE FINAL ANNOTATED AGENDA AND THE PROPOSED AGENDA FOR FINAL CHECK-IN CALL
- ✖ HOLD FINAL CHECK-IN CALL

The Co-Design Process usually includes two Co-Design Meetings, in person or via teleconference, plus a final check-in call. While it may vary from project to project, the timeline for the Co-Design Process generally follows the guidelines below:

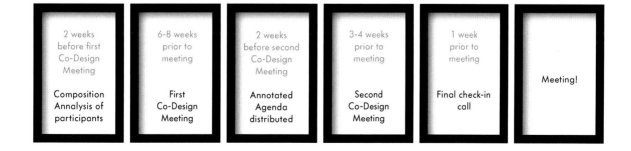

It is useful to start the Co-Design Process by having the organization that is sponsoring the meeting complete a "Composition Analysis" of participants. Using a matrix format, this analysis provides relevant information about the meeting participants, such as their position and role in the organization, to whom they report, ethnic or racial identification, Meyers-Briggs Type Indicator (MBTI) results, and key considerations relevant to the meeting at hand (e.g., relationships, resources, group dynamics, etc.). By glancing at the Composition Analysis (for an overview), or studying it (for a more in-depth understanding), all members of the Implementation Team can have a "picture" of the meeting participants to help with meeting preparation and execution — including, of course, all steps in creating the container for the meeting.[2]

SAMPLE FORMAT FOR PARTICIPANT COMPOSITION ANALYSIS

RESOURCES		RELATIONSHIPS AND RESULTS		RESOURCES
Person		Role	System	Influence, Impact, leverage
Name and characteristics MBTI, age, gender, race, ethnicity, language, photo if available	Professional background Area of study, experience	Title/role Authority regarding task related to meeting results or people attending the meeting	Organization and sector Accountability: to whom and for what	For each participant consider • Whom they can influence formally and informally • What they have direct control over • What they can make happen through connections and relationships • Their passion, values, commitment, knowledge • Points of potential conflict

Key Co-Design Steps

Another key element of the Co-Design Process is the Annotated Agenda, usually drafted by the facilitators of the meeting. The Annotated Agenda outlines in detail the conversation sequence, timing, tasks, and related materials for the meeting. It is, in fact, the principal document from which many of the container checklists are built, such as the lists of supplies and materials needed, as well as the travel times for staff and other logistics. Appendix Two provides a sample template for an Annotated Agenda.

A useful tool for the Co-Design Process is the "All-in-One Meeting Design Worksheet" included as Appendix Three of this booklet. Originally presented in *Introduction to Results Based Facilitation* by Jolie Bain Pillsbury, this worksheet provides a format for outlining your meeting results, building the agenda, and incorporating a composition analysis.

PREPARATION

While "Participant Preparation" occurs in some ways throughout the project, it is distinct enough in its purpose and importance to separate it out as a step in *Creating the Container to Achieve Results*. To ensure that participants become active participants, they need to have enough information to feel safe and grounded in the meeting plans. They need to be informed of meeting results, agenda, logistics, and other related items throughout the process so that they understand their roles, buy-in to the meeting's results and contribute to its success. Not to mention the fact that participants can more fully participate if they have had time to review the relevant materials and carry out requested preparatory work.

STEPS TO COMPLETE DURING PARTICIPANT PREPARATION

✖ SEND MEETING REMINDER AND RESULTS TO PARTICIPANTS

✖ SEND PUBLIC AGENDA AND PARTICIPANT PRE-WORK

✖ POST MEETING UPDATE ON SOCIAL MEDIA FORUMS, IF APPROPRIATE

✖ ORDER PARTICIPANT MATERIALS

✖ PREPARE PARTICIPANT MATERIALS

✖ ARRANGE FOOD FOR THE MEETING; POLL PARTICIPANTS FOR REQUESTS, IF NEEDED

✖ ARRANGE FOR NEEDED AUDIO-VISUAL EQUIPMENT

✖ ORDER MEETING SUPPLIES

While it may vary from project to project, the timeline for Participant Preparation generally follows the guidelines below:

Just after first Co-Design Meeting

Send meeting reminder and results to participants and post on social media

Just after second Co-Design Meeting

Order participant materials and meeting supplies

Just after second Co-Design Meeting

Arrange for food and AV equipment

2-3 weeks before the meeting

Send Public Agenda and participant pre-work

1-2 weeks prior to meeting

Prepare participant materials

Meeting!

Send Meeting Reminder and Results to Participants

After the meeting results are identified during the first Co-Design Meeting, send a meeting reminder to participants that lists the meeting results and other related information that is available at this point. The reminder should give enough information for participants to buy-in to being an active participant, as well as to make their travel plans for the meeting if they have not done so already.

Send Public Agenda and Participant Pre-Work

After the second Co-Design Meeting and about 2-3 weeks prior to the meeting, send a Public Agenda to the participants as well as any preparatory work they need to complete before the meeting. It is, of course, essential to allow enough time for the preparatory work to be done, as well as to include instructions. Often this requires sending related materials, such as articles or book excerpts, so keep that in mind when ordering participant materials.

The Public Agenda tracks very closely to the Annotated Agenda, in terms of results, topics of conversation, and timeframes. However, most of the supporting detail needed by the Implementation Team for meeting design, planning, and execution is left out — all of those details would certainly shock most participants!

Order and Prepare Participant Materials

For most meetings, creating the container involves preparing the participant materials in a way that holds everything together. This can include a meeting folder with your organization's identifying information on the front. Or, for longer workshops or more complex meetings, a binder with tabs separating the sections might be most appropriate. Whatever works for your meeting, make sure the materials are easy to access and include a table of contents for quick reference. Here are some items that we often include in participant folders or binders:

- Public Agenda
- Participant list, if appropriate
- Organizational chart
- Bios of facilitators and/or other staff
- Handouts of all data used in data walk
- Results-Based Accountability worksheets
- RBL Apps (short for applications)
  (the Apps can be downloaded and printed from: www.rbl-apps.com)
- Handouts
- Articles

For some meetings, you may have books or pamphlets to provide for reference and/or use during the meeting. It is best to provide these materials during the meeting to ensure that participants do not leave them at home.

Arrange Food for the Meeting

As we know from health-related literature, the type and timing of the food we eat is essential to our brain's functioning. Having healthy and abundant food also contributes to the participants' sense of comfort in the meeting on a psychological level, as well as the feeling of community in the space. Therefore, in most results-based meetings, we recommend that the food offerings include:

- Breakfast that includes protein (and, of course, caffeine);
- Snacks throughout the day, including having water available all day; and
- A protein-packed lunch with options for those with special dietary considerations (e.g., vegetarians, gluten-free, peanut allergy, etc.)

You may have to poll participants for their food requests and/or needs ahead of time.

Order Meeting Supplies

Having the right supplies in the room is essential to supporting the group in making progress toward a result! This is certainly a topic for which a "best practice" is to use a checklist each and every time. The following list is a comprehensive overview of supplies we normally need for RBL meetings. Feel free to add any additional items you prefer. Appendix Four provides this list with a column to check-off items as your order them, and it can be downloaded and printed from: www.rbl-apps.com.

OVERVIEW OF MEETING SUPPLIES[3]

PLACEMENT	ITEMS
On Participant and Implementation Team Tables	• Table toys — Two per participant
	• Candy or other snacks
	• Baskets — One each for table toys and candy
	• Mr. Sketch brand large point, chisel-tipped dark markers in contrasting colors (no red, which can signal critique)
	• Pads of paper
	• Pens
	• Name tents (with names printed on both sides)
	• Self-stick name tags
	• Journals or notepads, if appropriate
	• Hand sanitizer
	• Tissues
	• Post-it notes — 3x3 size; one pad per person of different colors
	• Binders or folders (as discussed above)
In the Room[4]	• Mr. Sketch brand large point, chisel-tipped dark markers in contrasting colors (no red)
	• Blue "painters" tape
	• Post-it notes — 4x6 size; one pad per person of different colors
	• Scissors
	• Stapler
	• 3-hole punch
	• Paper clips
	• Binder clips
	• Rubber bands
	• Extension cord(s)
	• Power strip(s)
	• Scotch tape
	• Portable printer or access to network printer
	• Self-stick easel pads — One for each flip chart stand plus 2 extra
	• Flip chart stands: One for each table and two up front
	• Books or pamphlets being provided

EXECUTION

After the many steps to prepare, it's time for the actual meeting, the phase we refer to as "Meeting Execution." It may seem on the surface that creating the container for results is over once the meeting begins. However, the container is continuously created as the meeting progresses and almost always requires adjustments and "real-time" interventions throughout. The person in charge of creating the container for the meeting must be vigilant in watching the meeting's developments and responding in ways that support the group's progress on work toward a designated result. The meeting leaders or facilitators also will be doing their work to support the group, and all these roles together support meeting the desired outcomes.

STEPS TO COMPLETE DURING DURING MEETING EXECUTION

The Afternoon/Evening Before the Meeting

- SET UP THE FURNITURE AND EASELS IN THE MEETING ROOM
- PLACE PARTICIPANT MATERIALS ON TABLES
- HANG AND/OR PLACE DATA ON WALLS OR FLIP CHART STANDS

One Hour Before the Meeting

- MEET WITH THE IMPLEMENTATION TEAM TO REVIEW AGENDA AND GO OVER ANY UPDATES

During the Meeting

- HAVE HANDOUTS READY TO GO SO THEY ARE EASILY DISTRIBUTED DURING THE DESIGNATED MEETING SLOT
- DISTRIBUTE REAL-TIME MEETING NOTES, AS NEEDED
- ORGANIZE AND/OR NUMBER FLIP CHART PAGES FOR FUTURE REFERENCE AS YOU GO ALONG; PERHAPS TAKE PICTURES OF THE PAGES
- REPLACE SUPPLIES AS NEEDED, SUCH AS FLIP CHART PAPER, DRIED-OUT MARKERS, ETC.
- ADDRESS ISSUES THAT ARISE RELATED TO MEETING PROCESS AND/OR LOGISTICS
- MANAGE "EXTERNAL" ISSUES THAT CONCERN THE GROUP, SUCH AS WEATHER REPORTS, TRAFFIC PROBLEMS, ETC.

When the Meeting Ends

- BREAK DOWN THE MEETING ROOM AND PACK SUPPLIES AWAY
- DEBRIEF WITH IMPLEMENTATION TEAM

Set Up the Furniture and Easels in the Meeting Room

We discussed earlier (under "Selecting and Reserving the Meeting Space") the possible ways to set up the furniture for the meeting, depending on the group size. The person who develops the Annotated Agenda for the meeting will likely indicate on the agenda which set-up to use. It is also a good idea to ask that person and other members of the Implementation Team to help set up the room (or at least observe the set-up after it's ready) to ensure that it meets everyone's expectations and requests. Sometimes what was envisioned doesn't work in reality and/or team members want a different layout. Since these types of changes are always possible, it is best to get the room set up and ready to go the afternoon or evening prior to the meeting.

Place Participant Materials on Tables

There is nothing more welcoming upon entering a meeting room than seeing the room set up and ready to go, including having all the materials ready for the participants. This may include a binder or folder, books (if assigned), Public Agenda, and any other items identified for use by participants during the meeting. Here is an example of participant tables equipped and ready to go:

ILLUSTRATION OF MEETING CONTAINER SET UP AND READY TO GO!

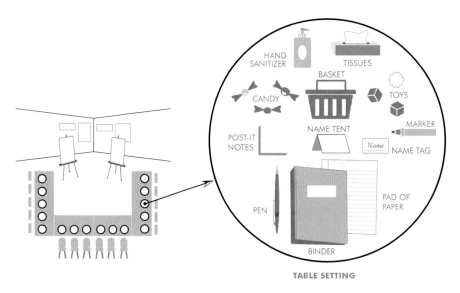

TABLE SETTING

Hang and/or Place Data on Walls or Flip Chart Stands

One of the most important pieces of the container for creating results is the data points that are placed in the meeting space. These data points, selected and developed by the meeting participants in consultation with the leaders and/or facilitators, represent the population-level result the group is working to impact as well as indicators related to that result. They might show trend lines and goals, or they might be more introductory in nature. Whatever their composition, it is critical that the group's meeting space include data relevant to the meeting result.

The data points are usually displayed in poster size and hung on the walls, if permitted, or placed on easel stands around the perimeter of the room. Participants often begin the meeting with a "Data Walk" where they review the posted data points, which stay up throughout the meeting. In doing RBL work, it is common also to have the Accountability Pathway hanging on the wall and other posters related to Results-Based Accountability. The Accountability Pathway can be downloaded from www.rbl-apps.com.

EXAMPLE OF DATA POSTERS PLACED IN ROOM

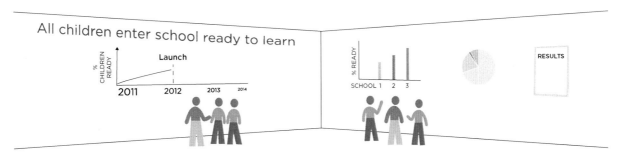

Copyright 2015 Sherbrooke Consulting, Inc.

Meet with the Implementation Team to Review Agenda and Go Over Any Updates

The Implementation Team usually gathers just before the meeting begins to review any updates, confirm their meeting roles, and touch base. The timing of this team gathering is usually about one hour prior to the meeting's start. It is important to be sure that all of the other pre-meeting steps have been completed by then.

Distribute Real-Time Meeting Notes, as Needed

It is sometimes helpful to the participants and their work to distribute in real-time the decisions made, proposals generated, or other content created during the meeting. Having the equipment necessary to pull this off is part of creating the container for results, as well as having staff available who can support this task. You can remind the group that this option is available — even before they ask — as part of the relentless focus on helping the group make progress toward the meeting result.

Organize and/or Number Flip Chart Pages for Future Reference

Another key part of creating the container for results is making sure the meeting is documented. This creates a summary for reference after the meeting to guide next steps, document action commitments, outline key proposals considered and decisions made, and other items. Groups will often appoint a meeting "documenter" to carry out this function. Most of the meeting summary will be extracted from the flip chart pages generated during the meeting.

It is much easier to compile the summary if the documenter and/or other participants work together to organize the pages as they go along. Sometimes numbering the pages is the best strategy, or taking pictures of the flips charts in the order that they are hanging. Whatever approach you use, remember that the pages are a key component to documenting the group's work, which is, in turn, a key component of creating the container to support them in meeting their results.

Manage External Issues That Concern the Group

When "external" issues, such as impending bad weather or rumors of traffic problems, distract the group, the participants can lose focus and make less progress while together. Creating the container can include, where needed, letting the group know that someone is monitoring the weather or other issues and will keep the group informed about them. This will free-up the participants to do the important work at hand.

Break Down the Meeting Room and Pack Supplies Away

While this step goes without saying, it is important to create a strategy for packing your supplies if you will have related additional meetings. Keeping needed meeting supplies and materials in one identified spot can ease the process of meeting again.

Debrief with Implementation Team

The Implementation Team always meets right after the meeting to go over how well the meeting results were met. This is a key time to bring up container-related issues that need to be changed, improved, or repeated in subsequent meetings. Also, the documenter can clarify any questions concerning next steps or assignments at this time, since they will be included in the meeting summary.

MEETING

FOLLOW-UP

As we stated earlier, creating the container for a meeting starts well before the meeting date and continues after its completion. Here are the typical follow-up steps groups need to execute to continue holding the container for the identified results:

STEPS TO COMPLETE DURING DURING MEETING FOLLOW-UP

✖   SEND ACTION COMMITMENTS TO PARTICIPANTS

✖   SEND FULL MEETING SUMMARY TO PARTICIPANTS

✖   POST MEETING RESULTS AND OUTCOMES ON SOCIAL MEDIA FORUMS, IF APPROPRIATE

✖   THANK MEETING SUPPORTERS, SUCH AS ONSITE ADMINISTRATIVE STAFF

✖   HOLD MORE IN-DEPTH DEBRIEF MEETING WITH IMPLEMENTATION TEAM, IF NEEDED

✖   SCHEDULE FOLLOW-UP MEETINGS, AS APPLICABLE

Most of these follow-up steps happen fairly soon after the meeting ends — and all are usually complete by two weeks or so after the meeting. Here is a general guideline on the timing of each step:

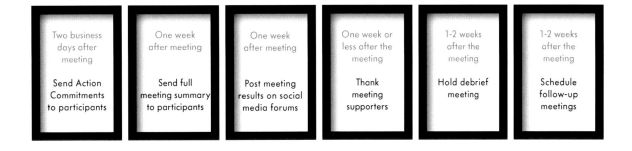

A key component of the theory of results-based leadership is that making public Action Commitments increases the likelihood of participants taking identified steps, which, in turn, impacts the likelihood of the group meeting its targeted results. Thus, creating the container for results also includes compiling and sending out participant Action Commitments just after the meeting date — usually within two business days.[5]

While the group may elect to use another format, here is a suggested format based on the work of many practitioners in the RBL community for structuring Action Commitments to have the greatest impact on aligning actions toward designated results:

Action(s)	With Whom	When	Contribution to the Result	Progress
For each action, write the steps needed to fully implement it.	Who will partner with you?	When will the action be completed?	How will actions contribute to making a measurable difference?	To be completed at the next session.
I will call the Director of the Housing Agency to set up a meeting to present our population-level results and request their participation in our project.	Participant X and Y	By the end of next week (March 6).	This will fill in the gap we have regarding including housing-related issues in our work.	

Send Full Meeting Summary to Participants

As noted above, making available a full meeting summary is an essential component of creating the container for results. Having a summary enables participants to refer to the decisions made, be held accountable for Action Commitments for themselves and others, and keep the work organized. All of this is in service of making progress toward the identified results, not as a way to check items off the list (although sometimes checking items off supports the progress toward results).

While the meeting summary can take various formats, we recommend that you include documentation of: (1) which proposed meeting results were accomplished or not, and (2) proposals made, discussion of those proposals, decisions made, and next steps. The format below is one that some groups use to document this proposal-based decision-making process:[6]

Proposal	Keith proposed that the strategic team needs to be the 6-plus option. The team members can be identified later, after we determine criteria for selecting members and criteria for success.
Decision	Proposal accepted by all
Next Steps	• Develop criteria for success and membership and a structure by mid-December • Sally will start the process by September 15 and send to team to review • Meet in mid-November to discuss

CLOSING

Creating the container to achieve results is an important part of supporting the work of any group, and, by extension, supporting the populations that the group's work is designed to serve. Creating the container requires focusing on the big picture while at the same time holding and tracking many details — a two-faceted task difficult for most people.

That is why we thought this booklet, *Creating the Container to Achieve Results*, would help. It provides a broad overview of the process, plus the detailed checklists you need to get it all done. That way, you can feel confident and enjoy the work of meeting with colleagues in service of creating important results. We wish you well in your work.

1 *This concept is quite integral to RBL; for more information on B/ART, see* Results Based Facilitation: Moving from Talk to Acton, Book One.

2 *To learn more about Composition Analysis, consult* Results Based Facilitation: Moving from Talk to Action, Book One. *The sample we provide is taken from that source.*

3 *Thanks to Ann Jackson and Maureen Pritchard for tips on this list based on their experience with the Annie E. Casey Foundation.*

4 *Depending on the group size and planned work activities, you might want to have two or more of some of these items, including blue tape, scissors, stapler, extension cord, and power strip.*

5 *For more information on Action Commitments and their relationship to accountability, see* Results Based Facilitation: Moving from Talk to Action, Book Two.

6 *For more information on Proposal-Based Decision Making, see* Introduction to Results Based Facilitation.

APPENDIX ONE

Download and print from www.rbl-apps.com

ITEM	COMPLETE?
Steps to Complete at Project Launch	
Set meeting date(s)	
Identify meeting staffing	
Get staff contracts in place, if applicable	
Identify members of the Implementation Team and clarify roles	
Reserve meeting space, including the afternoon before the meeting so the room can be set up	
Send "save the date" email to meeting participants	
Post meeting date and purpose on social media forums, if appropriate	
Arrange travel logistics for meeting staff: • Research, propose, and purchase travel tickets • Reserve hotel rooms • Reserve rental cars	
Set up a shared file system, if appropriate	
Set dates for two Co-Design Meetings and final check-in call	
Steps to Complete During Co-Design	
Provide template for participant Composition Analysis	
Send Proposed Agenda for first Co-Design Meeting with supporting materials, if any	
Hold the first Co-Design Meeting	
Send the draft Annotated Agenda to Implementation Team and the Proposed Agenda for second Co-Design Meeting	
Hold the second Co-Design Meeting	
Send the final Annotated Agenda and the Proposed Agenda for the final check-in call	
Hold final check-in call	

APPENDIX ONE continued

ITEM	COMPLETE?

Steps to Complete During Participant Preparation

Send meeting reminder and results to participants

Send Public Agenda and participant pre-work

Post meeting update on social media forums, if appropriate

Order participant materials

Prepare participant materials

Arrange food for the meeting; poll participants for requests, if needed

Arrange for needed audio-visual equipment

Order meeting supplies

Steps to Complete During Meeting Execution

The Afternoon/Evening Before the Meeting:

   Set up the furniture and easels in the meeting room

   Place participant materials on tables

   Hang and/or place data on walls or flip chart stands

One Hour Before the Meeting:

   Meet with the Implementation Team to review agenda and go over any updates

During the Meeting:

   Have handouts ready to go so they are easily distributed during the designated meeting slot

   Distribute real-time meeting notes, as needed

   Organize and/or number flip chart pages for future reference as you go along; perhaps take pictures of the pages

   Replace supplies as needed, such as flip chart paper, dried-out markers, etc.

   Address issues that arise related to meeting process and/or logistics

   Manage "external" issues that concern the group, such as weather reports, traffic problems, etc.

When the Meeting Ends:

   Break down the meeting room and pack supplies away

   Debrief with Implementation Team

Steps to Complete During Meeting Follow-Up

Send Action Commitments to participants

Send full meeting summary to participants

Post meeting results and outcomes on social media forums, if appropriate

Thank meeting supporters, such as onsite administrative staff

Hold more in-depth debrief meeting with Implementation Team, if needed

Schedule follow-up meetings, as applicable

APPENDIX TWO

SAMPLE ANNOTATED AGENDA

NAME OF ORGANIZATION

Leadership Team Meeting
Date
Location

ANNOTATED AGENDA

Meeting Results:
By the end of the meeting, participants will:
*
*

Meeting Preparation:
* Read…
* Bring…
* Consider…and write your answers to the following questions:

TIME	CONVERSATIONS	ANNOTATED ACTIVITIES/NOTES
Meeting Date – Day One		
8:00 am	Implementation Team Check-In	List supplies List room set up List handouts List data walk posters List other
Time	Task	Related notes
Meeting Date – Day Two		
8:00 am	Welcome and Check-In *Result:*	Related notes
Time	Task *Result:*	Related notes
Time	Task *Result:*	Related notes
Time	Task *Result:*	Related notes

APPENDIX THREE

ALL-IN-ONE MEETING DESIGN WORKSHEET

Download and print from www.rbl-apps.com

ALL-IN-ONE AGENDA
Come with meeting results in mind and leave with Action Commitments in hand

Meeting Title:

Date & Time:

Location:

MEETING PURPOSE

Meeting results	Accomplished	Some Progress	Not Addressed	Next Steps
Ready to work together				

Action Commitments made

AGENDA

Time	Task/Result	Notes: Insights, Decisions, Next Steps
	Task: Welcome, purpose, check-in Result: Ready to work together	
	Task: Result:	
	Task: Result:	
	Task: Check-out Result: Action Commitments made	
	Adjourn	

LEAVE WITH ACTION COMMITMENTS

Who needs to take action?	What actions will move the group forward?	When will the process start and end?	Why is this action a priority?

AGENDA, PAGE 2

Meeting Title:

Date & Time:

Location:

NOTES

COMPOSITION ANALYSIS

Name	Organization	Role	Contribution/Connection

APPENDIX FOUR

MASTER CHECKLIST FOR MEETING SUPPLIES

Download and print from www.rbl-apps.com

PLACEMENT	ITEMS	ORDERED?
On Participant and Implementation Team Tables	• Table toys — Two per participant	
	• Candy or other snacks	
	• Baskets — One each for table toys and candy	
	• Mr. Sketch brand large point, chisel-tipped dark markers in contrasting colors (no red, which can signal critique)	
	• Pads of paper	
	• Pens	
	• Name tents (with names printed on both sides)	
	• Self-stick name tags	
	• Journals or notepads, if appropriate	
	• Hand sanitizer	
	• Tissues	
	• Post-it notes — 3x3 size; one pad per person of different colors	
	• Binders or folders	
In the Room	• Mr. Sketch brand large point, chisel-tipped dark markers in contrasting colors (no red)	
	• Blue "painters" tape	
	• Post-it notes — 4x6 size; one pad per person of different colors	
	• Scissors	
	• Stapler	
	• 3-hole punch	
	• Paper clips	
	• Binder clips	
	• Rubber bands	
	• Extension cord(s)	
	• Power strip(s)	
	• Scotch tape	
	• Portable printer or access to network printer	
	• Self-stick easel pads — One for each flip chart stand plus 2 extra	
	• Flip chart stands: One for each table and two up front	
	• Books or pamphlets being provided	

APPENDIX FIVE

DETAILS FOR ORDERING
SELECTED MEETING SUPPLIES

MATERIALS	SOURCE AND/OR DESCRIPTION
Table Toys	www.officeplayground.com/Stress-Relievers-C33.aspx Two toys per participant
Name Tents	www.avery.com/avery/en_us/Products/Cards/Tent-Cards/Laser-and-Ink-Jet-Tent-Cards_05305.htm Avery or equivalent
Dark Markers	www.officemax.com/brands/mr-sketch/product-prod3640290
Self-Stick Easel Pads	www.staples.com/Staples-Stickies-25-x-30-Easel-Pads-White-2-Pack/product_573058
Participant Binders	www.amazon.com/Avery-Flexi-View-Binders-1-5-Inch-17637/dp/B006TIM1IG

ACKNOWLEDGMENTS

The framework for and components of *Creating the Container to Achieve Results* represent a smorgasbord of experiences gained through many engagements involving many people — which is, of course, the best way to get that just-perfect flavor! Many of the engagements were sponsored by the Annie E. Casey Foundation — an organization with which we have been so happy to collaborate. We have benefited, also, from partnerships formed through the Results Based Leadership Consortium, whose members have individually and collectively birthed, tried out, and polished many aspects of what it takes to create the container.

Upon reflection, this booklet represents what will likely become a "snapshot" of the work of *Creating the Container to Achieve Results*, "to be continued," we hope, by many leaders, teams, practitioners, project managers, program assistants, and more! We hope that updates of the booklet will be prompted often by the input of those who value the work of results-based leadership and its application.

The redesign of this booklet was funded by the Annie E. Casey Foundation, and I thank them for their support. Thanks also to Shagas Design for the report design and illustrations.

I also want to give a special acknowledgment to Raj Chawla, my husband and Principal of The OCL Group. It was his vision to create this booklet, one of many ideas born from his magnetic power of seeing possibility.

Patton Stephens

ABOUT THE AUTHOR

Patton Stephens, Director of Operations and Client Services for The OCL Group, brings a unique combination of leadership development, project management, coaching, and writing skills to the work of helping create containers to achieve results. With degrees and/or training in Public Administration, Organization Development, Coaching, and Results Based Facilitation, Patton provides a role desperately needed in all projects: establishing a solid foundation upon which important work can happen. Patton relishes her work in the world of results-based leadership, which both in theory and application honors her long-standing approach of encouraging individuals and groups to reach for high-impact external goals in ways that also facilitate internal change — a two-tiered approach that ensures enduring success.

Made in the USA
Monee, IL
14 August 2021